McPhail, David

Where can an Elephant Hide?

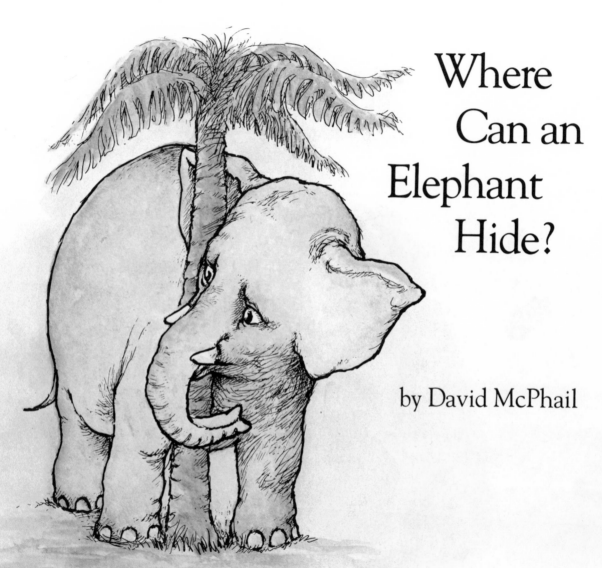

Where
Can an
Elephant
Hide?

by David McPhail

Doubleday & Company, Inc., Garden City, New York

LIBRARY OF CONGRESS CATALOGING IN PUBLICATION DATA

McPhail, David M.

    Where can an elephant hide?

    SUMMARY: The jungle animals help Morris the elephant
conceal himself from approaching hunters.

    [1. Elephants—Fiction.   2. Animals—Fiction]
I. Title.
PZ7.M2427Wh [E]

Library of Congress Catalog Number 78-31131
ISBN 0-385-12940-8 Trade
ISBN 0-385-12941-6 Prebound

For Jason

One day Morris the elephant was playing hide and seek with some of his friends. Morris didn't like playing hide and seek because he was always the first one found.

"We see you, Morris," said his friends.

"It's not fair," said Morris. "I'm too big. I don't have a place to hide."

Just then a bird flew down. "The hunters are coming!
The hunters are coming!" said the bird. "Everyone
hide!"

"Oh dear," said Morris. "There's no place I can hide."

"Don't worry," said a tiger. "If you lie down in the tall grass, the hunters won't see you. Watch me!"

When the tiger lay down in the grass, his stripes looked like shadows. The tiger seemed to disappear. But when Morris tried it, the other animals could still see most of him.

"Do I look like shadows?" asked Morris.

"No," they answered. "You look like an elephant lying in the grass."

"Oh, what will I do?" cried Morris. "I'm too big to hide!"

A monkey heard Morris and came to help.

"Just climb to the top of the tree," she said. "The hunters will never think to look for you there."

When the monkey climbed to the top of the tree, she was hidden by the leaves.

But when Morris climbed to the top of the tree, it bent all the way to the ground. And the leaves didn't hide him at all.

"This just won't do," said Morris.
"But thanks
any way."

Then a turtle spoke up. "Stay very still," he said, "and you'll look like a stone. Watch me!"

The turtle pulled his head and his legs and his tail into his shell and didn't move.

"It's amazing!" said Morris. "You look just like a stone!"

"Of course I do," said the turtle. "Now you try it!"

Morris pulled himself together as best he could and stayed very still. But no matter how still he stayed, he still looked like an elephant.

"Oh dear," he said. "The hunters are coming and I've nowhere to hide."

"It's easy to hide," said an ostrich. "Just bury your head in the sand as I do, and no one will be able to see you."

Morris dug a big hole and buried his head in it. After about a minute he pulled his head out and began coughing and sputtering.

"This won't do either," said Morris. "My mouth gets all filled with sand. And I can't breathe."

"It doesn't work anyway, you silly ostrich!" said the other animals. "We can still see both of you."

A baboon tried to be helpful. "You can hide in my cave," he said. "It's so dark in there the hunters will never see you."

But not all of Morris could fit into the baboon's cave. Only half of him could, and the half that couldn't looked very much like the back half of an elephant.

"What am I going to do?" sighed Morris. "The hunters are coming and I don't have a place to hide."

"I have a few feathers I don't need," said an old parrot. "Maybe if you wear them you'll look like a bird."

Morris rolled in some sticky mud, then jumped into the pile of feathers.

"There," he said, standing up. "How do I look?"

The other animals laughed and laughed. "You don't look like a bird at all," they said. "You look like an elephant with feathers."

Now Morris was very upset. He sat down and began
to cry.
"There, there," said the other animals. "We'll think
of something!"

They scraped off the mud and feathers, and all night long they sat with Morris, trying to think of a way for him to hide from the hunters. But no one could think of anything.

Along about dawn, the little bird came back again.

"The hunters are almost here," she said. "Why aren't you hiding?"

"We're trying to think of a way for Morris to hide," the animals answered.

"Follow me, Morris," said the bird. "I think I have the answer." Morris followed the bird to the river.

"Wade to the deepest part of the river and sit down," ordered the bird.

"If I do that, I'll drown!" protested Morris.

"If you breathe through your trunk you won't," the bird explained. "Now hurry ... the hunters are coming!"

Morris sat down, and not a moment too soon. For just then the hunters came paddling up in their canoe.

All the animals watched from their hiding places as the hunters paddled closer and closer to the spot where Morris sat with his trunk in the air.

The little bird flew out and landed on Morris's trunk, and when she did, her feathers tickled Morris and he sneezed. KERCHOO!

The hunters stopped and stared at the little bird, perched on what looked like a log sticking out of the water.

"Did you hear that bird sneeze?" asked one of the hunters.

"Yes," said the other hunter, "it sounded just like an elephant!"

Then they both laughed loudly and went on until they disappeared for good around a bend in the river.

All of the animals were very happy. And Morris was especially happy because he had finally found a place to hide. They danced and sang and laughed all day, and when the other animals were too tired to continue, Morris was still going strong.

"Let's play hide and seek," he shouted happily.